QUOTES FROM THE BOOK OF MORMON

Coloring book

BY SPIRITUAL GIFTS

THIS BOOK
BELONGS TO

....

INSTRUCTIONS

 Turn off your distractions. Relax and enjoy the spirit of the quotes and the peaceful nature of the pictures.

 Have fun! There is no wrong way to color, and with this book you are sure to have hours of relaxation and enjoyment, with the added benefit of inspiring quotes from the scriptures.

 This book works best with color pencils or markers. Wet mediums might bleed through. As images are printed one side only, you may place a piece of paper or card if you notice bleed through.

I WILL GO AND DO *what the* LORD HAS COMMANDED

1 Nephi 3:7

"By small means the Lord can bring about great things." 1 Nephi 16:29

Remember, remember that it is upon the rock of our Redeemer, who is Christ, the Son of God

that ye must build your foundation. Helaman 5:12

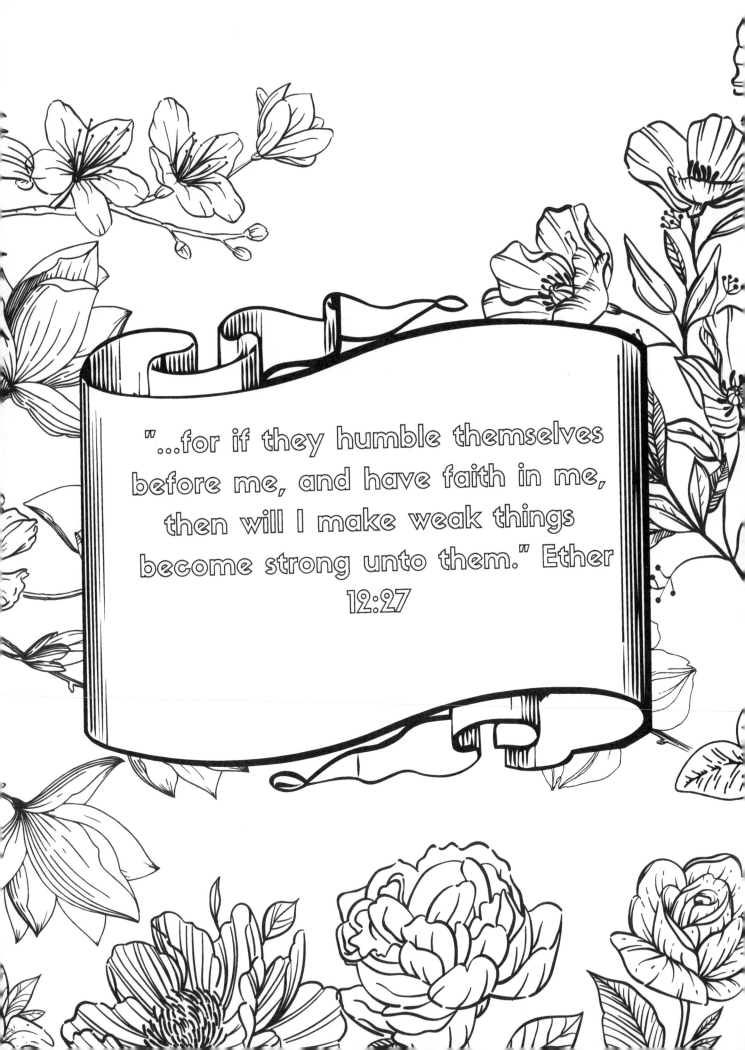

"...for if they humble themselves before me, and have faith in me, then will I make weak things become strong unto them." Ether 12:27

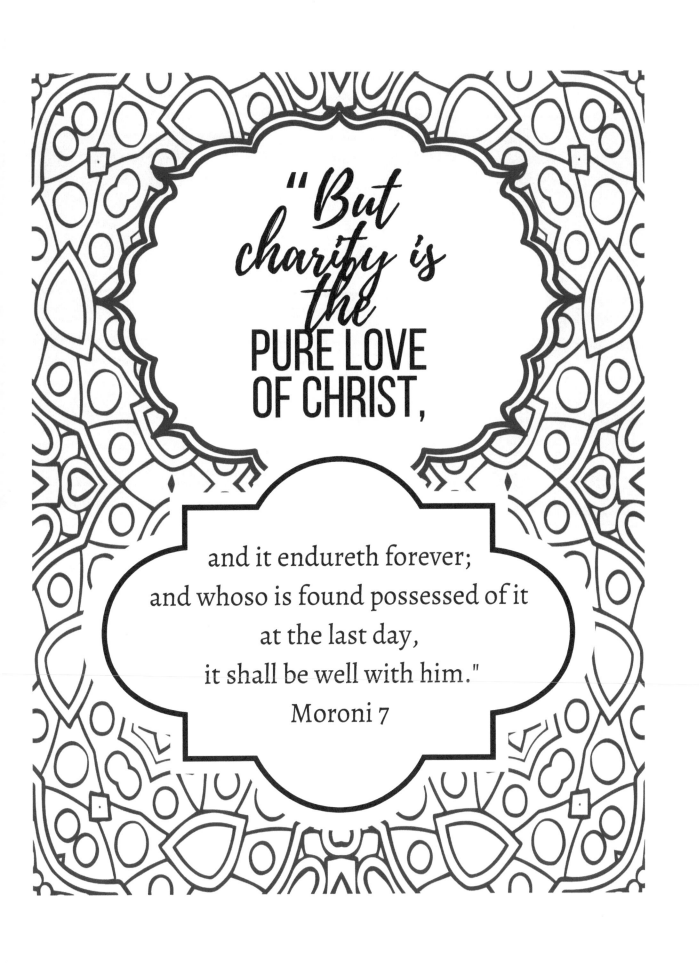

"But charity is the PURE LOVE OF CHRIST,

and it endureth forever;
and whoso is found possessed of it
at the last day,
it shall be well with him."

Moroni 7

"Adam fell that men might be; AND MEN ARE THAT THEY MAY HAVE JOY." 2 NEPHI 2:25

"And all thy children shall be taught of the Lord; and great shall be the peace of thy children."
3 Nephi 22:13

"But behold, I, Nephi,
will show unto you that the tender
mercies of the Lord are over
all those whom he hath chosen,
because of their faith,
to make them mighty
even unto the power of deliverance."
1 Nephi 1:20

"Yea, and cry unto God for all thy support; yea, let all thy doings be unto the Lord, and whithersoever thou goest let it be in the Lord; yea, let all thy thoughts be directed unto the Lord; yea, let the affections of thy heart be placed upon the Lord forever."
Alma 37:36

"yea, come unto Christ, ;

and be perfected in him, and deny yourselves of all ungodliness..."

Moroni 10:32

"...yea, even the earth,
and all things that are upon the face of it,
yea, and its motion, yea,
and also all the planets which move
in their regular form do witness
that there is a Supreme Creator.
Alma 30:44

"And see that all these things are done in wisdom and order; for it is not requisite that a man should run faster than he has strength." Mosiah 4:27

"Bear one another's burdens that they may be light..."

MOSIAH 18:8

"AND WE TALK OF CHRIST, WE REJOICE IN CHRIST, WE PREACH OF CHRIST, WE PROPHESY OF CHRIST, AND WE WRITE ACCORDING TO OUR PROPHECIES, THAT OUR CHILDREN MAY KNOW TO WHAT SOURCE THEY MAY LOOK FOR A REMISSION OF THEIR SINS."
2 NEPHI 25:26

"AND INASMUCH AS YE SHALL KEEP MY **COMMANDMENTS**, YE SHALL PROSPER, AND SHALL BE LED TO A **LAND OF PROMISE**; YEA, EVEN A LAND WHICH I HAVE PREPARED FOR **YOU**..."
1 NEPHI 2:20

"ye must pour out your souls in your closets, and your secret places, and in your wilderness."

Alma 34:26

"I came into the world
to do the will of my Father."
—3 Nephi 27:13

"...feast upon the words of Christ;
for behold,
the words of Christ will tell you
all things what ye should do."
2 Nephi 32:3

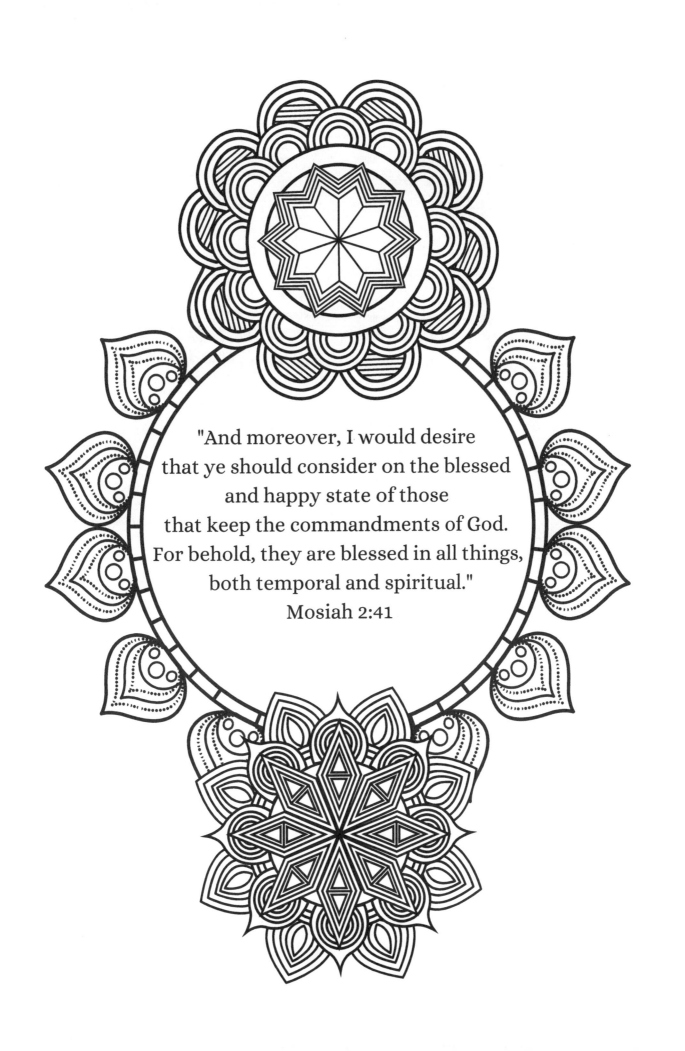

"And moreover, I would desire
that ye should consider on the blessed
and happy state of those
that keep the commandments of God.
For behold, they are blessed in all things,
both temporal and spiritual."
Mosiah 2:41

"IF YE HAVE

faith

ye can do ALL THINGS which are expedient unto
me."
Moroni 10:23